THE ULTIMATE MEN'S/WOMEN'S Two-Part CHOIR BOOK

14 CONTEMPORARY ARRANGEMENTS

ARRANGED BY JERRY NELSON

ALSO AVAILABLE:
C-3216N: Listening Cassette
TR-3216C: Stereo Track Accompaniment
TRS-3216C: Split-Track Accompaniment
C-3216S: Soprano Rehearsal Cassette
C-3216A: Alto Rehearsal Cassette
C-3216T: Tenor Rehearsal Cassette
C-3216B: Bass Rehearsal Cassette

BRENTWOOD PUBLISHING

© MCMXCV Brentwood Music Publishing, Inc.,
One Maryland Farms,
Brentwood, TN 37027.
All Rights Reserved. Unauthorized
Duplication Prohibited.

TABLE OF CONTENTS

Women's 2-part Arrangements:

Jubilate 3

How Beautiful 12

Favorite Song of All 25

In This Very Room 39

Love Will Be Our Home 47

Lamb of God 56

Praise You 64

Men's 2-part Arrangements:

For the Sake of the Call 72

Midnight Cry 84

More To This Life 95

Daystar 109

His Strength is Perfect 117

He's Been Faithful 126

The Basics of Life 134

Jubilate

Words and Music by
BABBIE MASON and CHERYL ROGERS
Arranged by Jerry Nelson

© Copyright 1990 Word Music (a div. of Word, Inc.)
All Rights Reserved. Used by Permission.

13
Ev-'ry - bod - y be glad. Raise your voice and make a joy-ful
Asus A D D/F♯
16
unis.
noise. Ju - bi - la - te! Shout for joy!
G Em D/F♯ GM7 A D
19
3rd time to Coda (bar 35)
Vs.1 (Solo or unison S.A.)
1. The
2. The
Vs.2 (Unison S.A.)
Em GM7 A
8vb

22
time has come for a cel - e - bra - tion.
sound of wor - ship is like no oth - er.
G/D D A D
22
25
Don't you feel the an - tic - i - pa - tion?
Lift your heart and de - light the Fa - ther,
Em7/D D Dsus D A Bm
25
28
Peo - ple have gath - ered from far and
with psalms and hymns and your spi - ri - tual
G/A G/D D Asus A
28

30
near. There's a rea - son to sing for God is
songs. Let the praise go on and
D D Em7/D D Em7/D D D/F♯
33
(both times)
(end solo)
1st time: Repeat to bar 11
2nd time: D.S. al Coda
(bar 11)
CODA
here.
on.
G A7/G Bm7 G/A GM7 A F♯/A♯
36
p legato
unis.
Al - le - lu - ia!
How good and how
Bm A/B Bm A/B Bm A/C♯
p
mp

39
div.
pleas - ant.
Al - le - lu - ia.
D
A/C♯
Bm
A/B
Bm
A/B
Bm
42
f
Praise the God of
earth and heav'n!
G/B
A/B
Bm A
G
A/G
Bm G
D
45
Ju - bi - la - te!
Shout for joy!
Ev - 'ry - bod - y be
D
A/D
D
D/F♯
D

glad._____ Raise your voice__ and make a joy-ful noise. Ju-bi-la-te! Shout for joy!_____ Ev-'ry-bod-y be glad._____

9

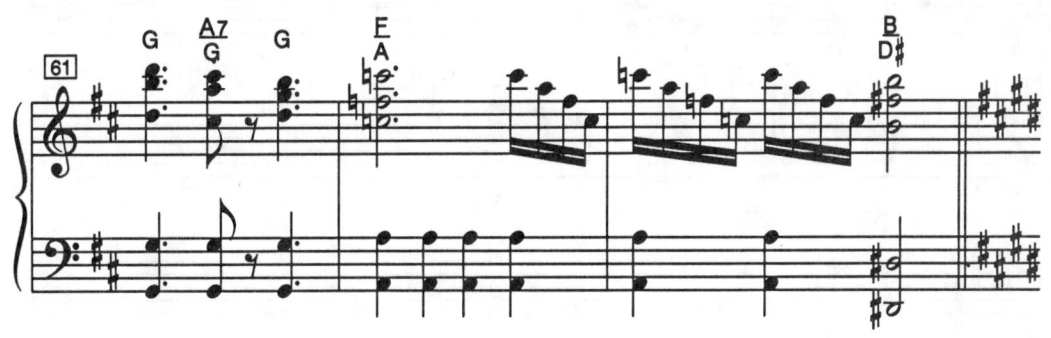

Lyrics:
Ju - bi - la - te! Shout for joy!
Ev - 'ry - bod - y be glad.
Raise your voice and make a joy - ful noise!

Ju - bi - la - te! Shout for joy!

Shout for joy!

How Beautiful

Words and Music by
TWILA PARIS
Arranged by Jerry Nelson

(♩ = ca.106)
Tenderly

SOPRANO/ALTO (Unison)

How

beau - ti - ful the hands that served the

© Copyright 1993 Ariose Music (a div. of Star Song Communications) ASCAP
and Mountain Spring Music/ASCAP.

13

wine and the bread and the sons of the earth. How beau-ti-ful the feet that walked the long, dust-y roads and the hill to the cross. How beau - ti - ful, how beau - ti - ful, how beau - ti - ful is the bod-y of

slight rit.

15

16

beau - ti - ful, how
how beau - ti - ful,

beau ti - ful is the bod-y of
how beau - ti - ful is the bod-y of

Christ. And as He laid down His
Christ.

life, we of-fer this sac - ri - fice: that we will live just as He died, will-ing to pay the price.

19

Will-ing to pay the price.

rit.

a tempo *div.*

How beau-ti-ful the ra-di-ant Bride, who waits for her Groom with His light in her eyes. How beautiful when humble hearts give the fruit of pure lives, so that others may live. How beautiful, How beauti-

55
how beau - ti - ful,
ful, how beau - ti -
A♭ B♭ A♭/C B♭/D
55
57
how beau - ti - ful
ful, how beau - ti -
A♭/C E♭ A♭/C B♭/D
57
59
unis.
is the bod - y of Christ.
ful is the bod - y of Christ.
A♭/C B♭/D Csus C
59

22

How beau-ti-ful the feet that bring the sound of good news and the love of the King. How beau-ti-ful the

67
hands that serve the wine and the bread and the
B♭ F/A B♭ F/A
67
69
sons of the earth. How beau - ti - ful,
How beau - ti -
B♭ C B♭/D F/A
69
71
how beau - ti - ful,
ful, how beau - ti -
B♭ C B♭ C/E
71

ful,_____ how__ beau - ti - ful__
how beau - ti -

ful is the bod-y of Christ.___
ful is the bod-y of Christ.___

Oo

Favorite Song of All

Words and Music by
DAN DEAN
Arranged by Jerry Nelson

© Copyright 1992 Dawn Treader Music (a div. of Star Song Communications) SESAC.

and He loves to hear the rain-drops as they splash to the ground in a mag-ic mel-o-dy.

He smiles in sweet ap-prov-al as the

27

waves crash to the rocks in har - mo - ny;

and cre - a - tion joins in u - ni - ty— to

sing to Him ma - jes - tic sym - pho - nies.

28

But His fav-'rite song of all

is the song of the re-deemed,

when lost sin-ners now made clean

29

lift their voic-es loud and strong.

When those pur-chased by His blood

lift to Him a song of love,

there's noth-ing more He'd rath-er hear,— nor so pleas-ing to His ear—

as His fav-'rite song of all.

And He loves to hear the an-gels as they

38
"Ho-ly, ho - ly!
sing: "Ho - ly, ho - ly is the Lamb."
A/D D G/D
40
Ho - ly is His name."
And heav - en's choirs in har - mo - nies
D G/D D D G/D
42
"Al - le - lu - ia!
lift up prais - es to the great "I Am."
A/D A Bm7/A A

32

new-born soul sings, "I've been re-deemed."

'Cause His fav-'rite song of all.

(end solo)

D.S. al Coda (to bar 21) **CODA**

It's not just mel-o-dies and har-mo-nies that

34

[56] not just clev-er lines— and phras-es that caus-es catch-es His— at-ten-tion,

G   Bm

[58] Him to stop— and lis-ten; but when an-y heart set free, washed and

Em

[60] bought by Cal-va-ry,— be-gins to sing...

sfz

Asus

35

it's His fav-'rite song of all.

A E G#m7 A

It's the song of the re-deemed,

C#m

when lost sin-ners now made clean

B Bsus

lift their voic-es loud and strong.

When those pur-chased by His blood

lift to Him a song of love,

37

81
Lamb.
Al - le - lu - ia! O Al - le - lu - ia!
81
83
Holy is the
Ho - ly!
83
85
Lamb!
Al - le - lu - ia! O Al - le - lu - ia!
85

In This Very Room

Words and Music by
RON HARRIS
Arranged by Jerry Nelson

11
(If using soloist,
S.A. "oo" here)
joy for one like me.
Oo
And there's quite e-nough hope and
Bm7
A
A
B7
F♯
14
quite e-nough pow - er to chase a-way an-y
Oo
F7
A
E
16
gloom, for Je - sus, Lord Je - sus
D♯m7♭5
A
E
F♯m

41

ALL is in this ver-y room.
is in this ver-y room.

(Altos) *mp* And in this ver-y room

there's quite e-nough love for all of us; And

42

(Sop.) Oo— in this ver-y room there's quite e-nough joy for all of us. And there's quite e-nough hope and quite e-nough pow-er to chase a-way an-y

43

44

*Soloist may sing melody to end.

joy_____ for all the world._ And there's quite e-nough hope and quite e-nough pow-er___ to chase a-way an-y gloom, for Je-sus, Lord

58
p
Je - sus
is
is
Gm
E♭M7
Fsus
58
61
in this ver - y room,
in this ver - y room,
B♭
E♭M7
61
p
63
rit.
(9)
in this ver - y room.
in this ver - y room.
B♭
E♭M7
B♭2
63
rit.

Love Will Be Our Home

Words and Music by
STEVEN CURTIS CHAPMAN
Arranged by Jerry Nelson

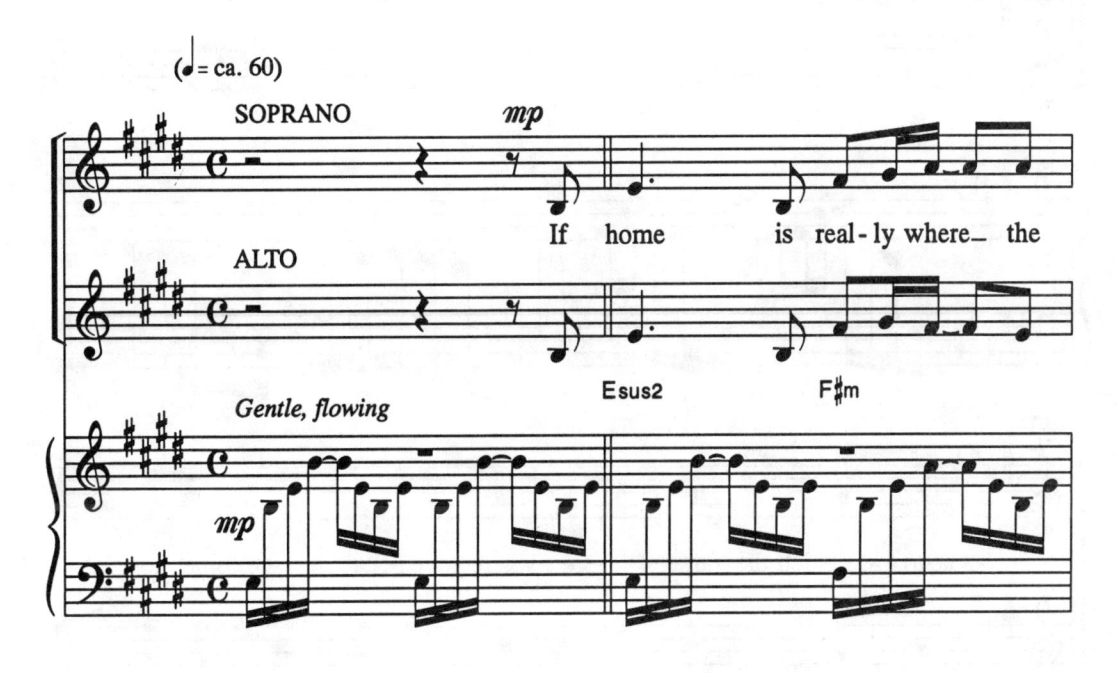

share. For e-ven with our diff'-renc-es, our hearts are much the same; for where love is,— we come to-geth-er there._____ Wher'-ev-er there- is laugh-ter ring-ing, some-one smil-ing, some-one dream-ing, we can live to-geth-er there.

Love will be our home. Wher-ev-er there are chil-dren sing-ing.
Love will be our home, Oo

where a ten-der heart is beat-ing, we can live to-geth-er there, 'cause
(oo)

love will be our home.

(opt. S.A.) Love will be our home. With love our hearts can be a fam-'ly, and hope can bring this fam-'ly face to

(opt. Solo) A fam-'ly of hope. Oo

17
love will be our home.
17
F♯m7 Bsus7 E
19
(opt. Solo)
(opt. S.A.)
With love our hearts can be a
Love will be our home.
19
F Gm
21
fam - 'ly, and hope can bring this fam- 'ly face to
A fam - 'ly of hope. Oo
21
C7 F B♭ C7/B♭

face. And though we may be far a-part, our
Oo (words)

hearts can be as one when love brings us to-geth-er in one

place. (Solo out) Wher-ev-er there is laugh-ter ring-ing,

someone smil-ing, some-one dream-ing, we can live to-geth-er there.

Love will be— our home. Where there are words— of kind-ness spo-ken,

where a vow is nev-er bro-ken, we can live to-geth-er there.

53

54

Love will, love will be our home.
Love, love, love, love will be our

D C² C G

Love will, love will be our home. Wher-
home. Love will be our home.

D C Em D/F#

ev-er there is laugh-ter ring-ing, some-one smil-ing, some-one dream-ing,

G D/F# Em G/D

55

Lamb of God

Words and Music by
TWILA PARIS
Arranged by Jerry Nelson

Your on-ly Son, no sin to hide; but You have sent Him from Your side to walk up-

© Copyright 1985 Straightway Music (a div. of Star Song Communications) ASCAP
and Mountain Spring Music.

on this guilt-y sod, and to be-come the Lamb of God.

Your Gift of Love they cru-ci-fied.
Your Gift of Love, cru-ci-fied.

They laughed and scorned Him as He
They laughed and scorned as He

died. The hum-ble King they named a fraud, and sac-ri-ficed the Lamb of God. O Lamb of God! Sweet Lamb of

God! I love the ho-ly Lamb of God. O wash me
Lamb of God,___ Lamb of God.___ O

C/E C G/B Am F C/E Gsus G G7/F

in His pre-cious blood; my Je-sus Christ, the Lamb of
wash me in His pre-cious blood. Christ, the Lamb of

Am FM7 Em Am G FM7 C/G G7

God.
God.

C Am F G Am G Em

33
Am F G Am G Em
35
Am F G Am G Em
37
unis.
f Stronger
I was so
37
Am F G Am G Em
Fm B♭m G♭M7
40
lost, I should have_ died; but You have brought me to Your
D♭ G♭ A♭ D♭ A♭/C B♭m G♭M7 D♭/F
40
f

43
div.
side to — be led by Your staff and rod, and — to be
Absus Ab Ab7/Gb Bbm GbM7 Db Bbm GbM7
43
46
called a lamb of God. O — Lamb of
O — Lamb of
Db/Ab Absus Db
46
48
God! Sweet — Lamb of God! I love the
God! —, Sweet Lamb of God!
Bbm GbM7 Ab7/Gb Db/F Db Ab/C
48

ho - ly Lamb of God. O wash me
Ho - ly Lamb of God. O wash me

in His pre - cious blood 'til I am

just a lamb of God. O wash me

in His pre-cious blood, my Je-sus Christ, the Lamb of God.

Praise You

Words and Music by
ELIZABETH GOODINE
Arranged by Jerry Nelson

life praise You. Praise

You, praise You; Let my

life, O Lord, praise You. Praise
Praise

You, O Lord, praise You; Let my
You, O Lord, praise You; Let my

life praise You. Praise
life, O Lord, praise You. Praise

You, praise You; Let my
You, O Lord, praise You; Let my

life, O— Lord, praise— You.— Lord, I
life,— O— Lord, praise— You.—

come to— You to - day— with a
I— come with a sim - ple

sim - ple— pray'r to— pray:— In—
pray'r. Oo—

25
ev - 'ry-thing I do let my
In ev - 'ry-thing Lord, that I do, let my
Gm Em7♭5 F7sus4 F7/A B♭/D
25
27
D.S. al Coda (to bar 13)
life, O Lord, praise You. Praise
life, O Lord, praise You. Praise
E♭ Cm7 B♭/F F7 B♭sus B♭ B♭/D
27
D.S. al Coda (to bar 13)
29
CODA
(S.)
You. Lord, You
You.
B♭sus B♭7/A♭ G♭M7 E/F♯ B/D♯
29
CODA
f

69

formed me out of clay; For your glory I was made. (A.) Now use this vessel as You choose; Let my
ves - sel as You choose.

life, O— Lord, praise— You.———————— Praise—
O— Lord,— praise You.———————— Praise—

You, praise You;———————— Let my
You,— O— Lord,— praise— You;———————— Let my

life praise— You.———————— Praise—
life, O— Lord, praise You.———————— Praise—

* if desired, add Solo on mel. (freely) with Sopranos to end.

For the Sake of the Call

72

Words and Music by
STEVEN CURTIS CHAPMAN
Arranged by Jerry Nelson

(♩ = ca.112)
Robust, energetic

TENORS
We will a-ban-don it all for the sake of the call.

BASSES
We will a-ban-don it all.

No oth-er rea-son at all, but the sake of the call.

No oth-er rea-son at all.

© Copyright 1990 SparrowSong, a div. of The Sparrow Corp./Greg Nelson Music
(adm. by The Copyright Co., Inc.)/Careers-BMG Music Publishing.

73

Whol- ly de- vot- ed to live and to die for the sake of the call.

No- bod- y stood and applaud-ed them,___ so they knew from the start this road would not lead to fame.___ All they real-ly knew_ for sure was Je-sus had called to them. He said,

75

76

lieve and none could ex-plain:___ How some
water can-not help but flow.___ Once we
cra-zy fish-er-men a-greed to go where Je-sus led, with
hear the Sav-ior's call,___ we'll fol-low wher-ev-er He leads be-
no thought for what they could gain, for Je-sus had called them by
cause of the love He has shown; be-cause He has called us to

51
TENORS
name. (end solo) All enter And they an-swered: We will a-
f BASSES
go, we will an-swer: We will a-
Ab Bb Eb Fm7 Eb/G
ff
54
ban-don it all for the sake of the call.
ban-don it all.
Bb/C Cm Ab Ab/Bb
3
57
sim.
No oth-er rea-son at all, but the
No oth-er rea-son at all.
Eb Fm7 Eb/G Cm Ab

sake of the call. Whol-ly de-vot-ed to live and to die for the sake of the call.

(repeat to bar 37)

69 (T.)
die. Not for the sake of a creed or a cause,
(B.)
A♭ B♭/A♭ Gm7 E♭/G
mf
72
Not for a dream or a prom - ise;
Sim-ply be-cause it is
Fm7 A♭ B♭ B♭/A♭
75
Je - sus who calls, and if we be-lieve we'll o - bey.
sfz
Cm A♭ E♭/G B♭/F E♭ D♭
f

78
f
We will a - ban - don it
We will a - ban - don it
B♭
E♭
ff
81
sim.
all for the sake of the call. No oth - er
sim.
all. No oth - er
Fm7
B♭/D
E♭
Fm7
E♭/G
f
8vb
84
rea - son at all but the sake of the call.
rea - son at all.
B♭/C
Cm
E♭/B♭
A♭
Fm7
B♭/D
8vb

81

We will abandon it all for the sake of the call. No other reason at all but the sake of the call. Wholly devoted to live and to die for the sake of the call. Wholly devoted to live and to die for the

83

sake — of the

call!

Midnight Cry

Words and Music by
DAVE CLARK and FELICIA SHIFLET
Arranged by Jerry Nelson

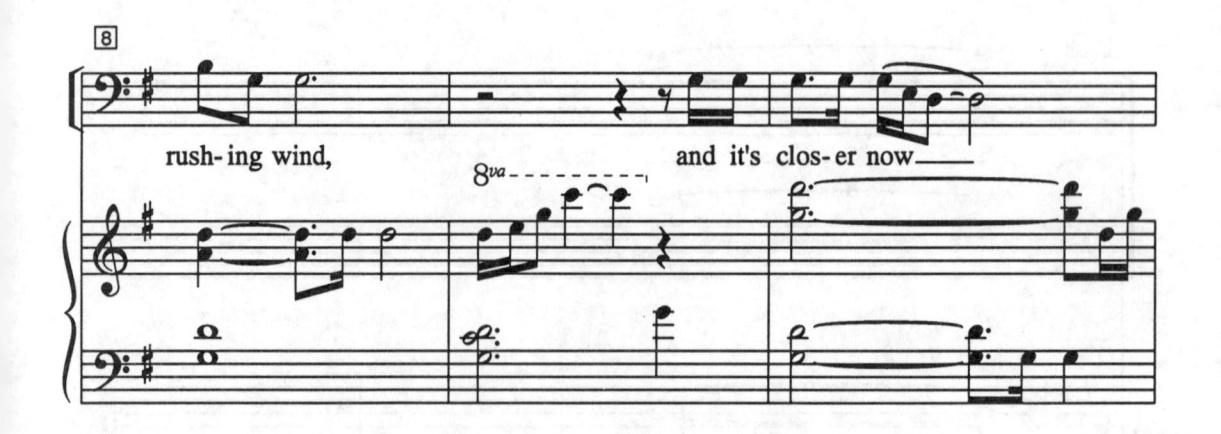

Very free style and tempo

SOLO *Breathy, mysteriously*

I hear the sound of a might-y, rush-ing wind, and it's clos-er now

© 1986 Trail Gospel Music.
All rights reserved. Used by permission.

than it's ev - er been.___ I can al-most hear the trum-pet___ as Gab-riel sounds the call.___ At the mid-night cry___ we'll be go - in' home. Oh,___

86

29
I can al-most see the Fa-ther as He says: "Son, go get your
where. Oo
C/D G Bm C C/D
29
32
(2nd time)
unis.
chil - dren." At the mid-night cry
Go get your chil - dren.
Bm B/D♯ Em Cm2/E♭ Cm/E♭ G/D
32
35
ALL-both times
(T.)
the bride of Christ will rise. When Je-sus
(B.)
C/D G C/D
35

steps out_____ on a cloud to call His chil-dren,_____ the dead in Christ will rise_____ to meet Him__ in the air._____

45
And then those that re - main
Those that re -
Dsus7
G
Bm7
47
shall be quick-ly changed.
main
C
C/D
Bm
B7
2nd time to CODA
mf (bar 54)
49
At the mid-night cry
mid-night cry
Em
Cm2/E♭
Cm/E♭
G/D
(bar 54)

90

Soloist rejoins-ad lib.

At the mid-night cry, at the mid-night cry, when Jesus, Jesus, Jesus steps out on a cloud to call His children,

the dead in Christ will rise
to meet Him in the air.
And then those that re-main
Those that re-

main shall be quickly changed.

At the midnight cry, At the midnight cry,

at the midnight cry, at the midnight cry,

94

More To This Life

95

Words by
STEVEN CURTIS CHAPMAN

Music by
STEVEN CURTIS CHAPMAN
and PHIL NAISH
Arranged by Jerry Nelson

Vs.1 To-day I watched in si-lence as peo-ple passed me by, and I

(Vs.2) night he lies in si-lence, star-ing in-to space, and he

© Copyright 1989 Sparrow Song/New Wings Music (a div. of Lorenz Creative Services)/
Greg Nelson Music (BMI) Pamela Kay Music/Beckengus Music/L.C.S. Songs
(a division of Lorenz Creative Services) ASCAP.
Used by permission. All rights reserved.

strained to see if there was some-thing hid-den in their eyes;___ but they
looks for ways to make to-mor-row bet-ter than to-day;___ but
all looked back at me___ as if to say:___ "Life just_ goes
in the morn-ing light it looks the same:___ Life just_ goes
on." The
on. He

old familiar story just told in different ways:— Make the
takes care of his fam-'ly, he takes care of his work,— and
most of your own journey, from the cradle to the grave.—
ev-'ry Sunday morning he takes his place at the church;— And
Dream your dreams— tomorrow because today— life must— go
somehow he still feels the need to search.— Life must— go

19
ALL-both times (TENOR)
f
on.
But there's
(BASS)
on.
G
D
G/D
D7
21
more to this life than liv - ing— and
CM7
C6
Dsus
23
unis.
dy - ing, more than— just try-in' to make it thru the day.
Em
C
CM7
D

99

More to this life, more than these eyes a-lone can see; and there's more than this life a-lone can be.

31
Vs 2: SOLO or TENOR/BASS unison
D.S. al Coda
(to bar 5)
Vs.2
To-
31
C
C6
CM7
D.S. al Coda
(to bar 5)
33
CODA
(SOLO or TENORS)
mf
But where do we start to
(ALL or BASSES)
Where do we
G
33
CODA
Am7
35
find ev - 'ry part of what makes this life com -
3
find part of what makes this life com -
35
Bm7
C

plete? If we'll turn our eyes to
plete? If we'll turn our
Je-sus, we'll find life's true be-gin-ning is
eyes, we'll find life's true be-gin-ning is
there at the cross, where He died.
there at the cross, where He died.

102

More to this life, more than these eyes a-lone can see; And there's more to this life than liv-ing and dy-ing, more than just try-in' to make it thru the day. More to this life, more than these eyes a-lone can see; and there's more than this life a-lone can be.

105

106

life.

More to this
More than

life.
tryin' to make it thru another day.

More to this life. More than this life alone can be.

Oo

ritard

Daystar

Words and Music by
STEVE RICHARDSON
Arranged by Jerry Nelson

(♩ = ca. 60)
With great emotion

[4] SOLO or T.B. unison

Li-ly of the Val-ley, let your sweet a-ro-ma fill my life. Rose of Sha-ron, show me

© Copyright 1988 Ariose Music (a div. of Star Song Communications) ASCAP.

110

how to grow in beau-ty in God's sight.

Fair-est of Ten Thou-sand, make me a re-flec-tion of Your light. Day-star, shine down on me; Let Your love shine thru me in the night. (ALL:)

21
(T.)
mp
Lead me, Lord, I'll fol-low an-y-where You o-pen up the
(B.)
B♭
(piano cues: on D.S.)
f
B♭
C7
23
door.
Let Your Word speak to me.
F
F7 G♭7 G7
26
Show me what I've nev-er seen be-fore.
Lord, I
G7
C
C9

wan-na be a wit-ness; You can take what's wrong and make it right. Day-star, shine down on me; Let your love shine thru me in the night. Lord, I see a world that's dying, wounded by the master of deceit; Groping in the darkness, haunted by the years of past defeat. But then I

see You stand-ing near me, Lord, shin-ing with com-pas-sion in Your
Oo

eyes. All-
Oo (wds.) I pray,

"Je-sus, shine down on me. Let Your love shine thru me in the

night." Oh, oh, oh,

D.S. al Coda (to bar 21)

night.

CODA

Day-star, shine down on me; Let Your love shine thru me in the
(mel.)

57
night.
Gradually slowing
F
Bbm
Gm7b5
Gradually slowing
59
rit.
unis.
Je-sus, shine down on me.
Let your love shine thru me in the
F
C
Gm
C7
rit.
61
night.
F
Bb
F
F2
rit.

His Strength Is Perfect

Words and Music by
STEVEN CURTIS CHAPMAN
and JERRY SALLEY
Arranged by Jerry Nelson

No great suc-cess to show,— no glo-ry on my own;— yet in my weak-ness He is there to let me know: His strength is

22
per - fect when our strength is gone.
when our strength is
Asus2/4 Am D/F♯ G C/G
25
gone. He'll car - ry us when we can't car - ry on.
G D/E Em Asus2/4 Am/G D/F♯
28
Raised in His pow - er the
Dm6/F E7 Asus2/4 Am/G

120

121

52
He hears our hum-ble cry, and proves a -
Em C G/B Asus4 A
55
D.S. al Coda (to bar 22)
CODA
gain His strength is per - fect,
(mel.)
Am D7 G Gsus2/4 G Asus4 Am/G
58
f
His strength is per - fect when our strength is when
(mel.)
F Bb/F F/Eb Bb/D Cm7 Cm/Bb F/A Fsus4 F

121

122

He hears our humble cry, and proves a-gain His strength is perfect, His strength is perfect when our strength when is

our strength is gone. He'll carry us when we can't
gone. carry on. Raised in His
power the weak become strong.

124

the weak be-come strong. His strength is per - fect,_____ His strength is per - fect.

He's Been Faithful

**Words and Music by
CAROL CYMBALA**
Arranged by Jerry Nelson

faith-ful — to me. When my
faith-ful — to me. The days I

strength was all gone, when my heart had no
spent so self-ish-ly, reach-ing out for what pleased

song, still in love, He's proved faith-ful — to
me— e-ven then, God was faith-ful — to

me. Ev-'ry word He's
me. Ev-'ry time I
prom-ised is true; what I
come back to Him, He is
tho't was im-pos-si-ble, I see my God
wait-ing with open arms, and I see once a-

129

Tho' in my heart I have ques-tioned, e-ven failed to be-lieve— yet He's been faith-ful, faith-ful to me.

48
(repeat to bar 6)
All-Unison (or opt. Solo)
Vs.2 When my
Fm7
B♭m7
E♭sus
(repeat to bar 6)
3
3
51
2
f
faith - ful, He's faith - ful. In my
He's faith - ful to me. In my
2 D♭/E♭
D/E
E♭9(♭5)
54
heart I have ques - tioned, e - ven failed to be -
DM7
G♯m7
C♯(♭9)
F♯m(add9)
F♯m7
f

lieve— yet He's been faith-ful, faith-ful.— In my heart I have ques-tioned, e-ven failed to be-lieve— yet He's been faith-ful, so

faith - ful to me. He's been faith - ful. When I
faith - ful to me.

failed Him, He was faith - ful. He's
He's so faith - ful, He's

Slowing...
faith - ful to me.

The Basics of Life

Words and Music by
MARK HARRIS and DAN KOCH
Arranged by Jerry Nelson

We've turned the page, for a new day has dawned; and we've re-ar-ranged what is right and what's

© Copyright 1992 Paragon Music Corp., A-Knack-For-This Music, Point Clear Music/ASCAP.
All Rights Reserved. Used by permission of Benson Music Group, Inc.

wrong. Somehow we've drifted so far from the truth that we can't get back home. And where are the virtues that once gave us light, and where are the morals that governed our lives? Someday we all will awake and look back just to find what we've lost.

We need to get back to the bas-ics of life, a heart that is pure and a love that is blind; a faith that is fer-vent-ly ground-ed in Christ; the hope that en-dures for all time.

These are the bas-ics; we need to get back to the bas-ics of life. The new-est

rage is to rea-son it out.___ Ya just med-i-tate and you can o-ver-come an-y doubt.___ Af-ter all, "man is a god,"___ they say God is no long-er___ alive. But I still believe in the old rugged cross, and I still believe there is hope for the lost; And I know the Rock of all ages will

141

stand thru the chang-es of time, thru the chang-es of time. life.

(opt. solo)
We've let the dark-ness in-vade us too long. We've got-ta

turn the tide.

We need the pas-sion that burned long a-go to come and o-pen our eyes— there's no room for com-pro-mise.

We need to get back to the bas-ics of life, a heart that is pure and a love that is blind. We need to get back to the bas-ics of life,— a heart that is— pure and a love that is blind;— a faith that is fer-vent-ly ground-ed in Christ;— the hope that en-dures for all

time. These are the bas-ics; we need to get back to the bas-ics. get back to the bas-ics of life. O woh, the bas-ics of

life. ____ We need to get back to the bas-ics of
life— faith, hope, love; bas-ics of
life. We need to get back to the bas-ics of life.

NOTES